WORKERS' COMPENSATION MADE SIMPLE,

WHAT EVERY BUSINESS SHOULD KNOW!

BY: Mark Kirby © 1993-2009

IMPORTANT: The author or publisher is not liable for any damages,

events, situations, or other results from the use of this

educational book. This publication is not a substitute for legal advice.

IMPORTANT! – READ THIS

This publication is based on general rules and is not meant

to be specific for your state or province. Workers'

Compensation is not identical in each state but there are

major similarities since they were all based on the same

"blueprint". **YOU MUST CHECK WITH YOUR STATE REGULATORY**

AGENCY OR CARRIER FOR SPECIFIC VERIFICATION OR INFORMATION

IF NEEDED.

This publication is for education only and is not meant to

be used to process claims or to file for specific benefits.

If used properly, this program should help you to understand the basic concepts of Workers' Compensation and how it is generally applied. Where applicable, ranges have been given for some benefits as examples only. Benefits may be higher or lower than those given depending on which state you are located. The program will also help teach you on ways to reduce your premium costs and reduce claim costs as the employer.

If you want to learn the Workers' Compensation Law for your specific state, you will need to study the Code of Laws for your state regarding Workers' Compensation Rules. For Premium questions, contact your State Insurance Department.

For more information on this publication, please contact:

EIC Research, Inc.

Attn: Mark Kirby

PO Box 6517

Columbia, SC. 29260-6517

TABLE OF CONTENTS

WHAT IS WORKERS' COMPENSATION:

Workers' compensation first started in Germany in the 1800's.

A need was seen to take care of injured workers so they did not

suffer physically or financially from injuries resulting from

working for a company. Workers' compensation became common in

the US in the 1930's and 1940's. It continues today in all 50

states and in territories. Workers' Compensation is similar in

Canada. Workers' compensation is basically the same and a change

in benefits in a particular state may result in similar changes

in other states. When workers' compensation was first proposed,

a compromise was reached between businesses and the worker.

In order to encourage businesses to accept full responsibility

for the premium costs of Workers' Compensation, the workers gave

up the right to sue the employer for damages resulting from a job

related injury. This "doctrine" continues basically intact to

this day. Rather than a benefit, workers' compensation is a

legally mandated right of the worker. Businesses who meet

certain requirements must provide workers' compensation for

all employees of the business. There are fines and other forms

of punishment for businesses (and owners) who have not provided coverage as required by law. Workers' Compensation is purchased

from several possible sources: Private companies, State Funds,

Insurance Pools, Self-Insurance Programs. Workers' compensation

Laws and regulations are made by each state and are regulated

by state officials. Workers' Compensation by itself may lose money

for carriers or not make enough profit, so some carriers may require a business

to purchase other coverage in addition to workers' compensation

before <u>voluntary</u> workers' compensation coverage is offered by

the insurance carrier. By shifting all of their insurance coverage to the

same carrier, a company with a bad experience modifier may be able to

obtain coverage outside of the assigned risk pool (more expensive!).

Most states require a notice to be posted in the workplace to

advise workers of their coverage for job related injuries. The posting

is similar to other displays required by the Federal Government

related to wage and hour benefits. The notice usually explains

what the basic benefits of workers' compensation are for in your

particular state and what state agency regulates Workers' Compensation.

The posting also explains whom to contact for information. Businesses should check with the regulatory officials to determine if a workers' compensation

poster is required. Failure to post any required information may result in a fine

for the business.

WHO IS COVERED:

Unless a business is NOT required to cover employees because they are exempt under Workers' Compensation rules all employees are covered. The Workers' Compensation coverage applies to part time employees, temporary employees (not from outside temporary source), full time employees, and special groups of volunteers (fire, police, paramedic) in some states. National guard military are also covered while performing **STATE** duties (check state rules) in some states.

An employee of a company is automatically covered from the very moment they start work. Independent contractors or consultants are usually not covered by the business they are working with. Casual employees (pick up labor, one day help, etc.) are not normally covered for job injuries. In some states prison inmates are covered in state, county, and city prisons PROVIDED they are on some type of work program either in the prison or on a work release program. Volunteers are covered in some areas but this is more the exception than the rule. People of all ages are covered in most areas and there is no limit with regard to how old or how young an employee is. Some states limit coverage for fire and police based on how long they have been on the job or whether or not they have had a recent physical as required by law.

Illegal aliens and migrant workers are sometimes covered depending on their job duties, this also needs to be checked in your state.

Family members who do not work for a company are not covered by the spouse or parent's workers' compensation coverage.

WHEN EMPLOYEES ARE COVERED:

The first day, the first minute a person begins work they
are covered. There is no waiting period as with some health
insurance plans or disability plans. To receive benefits for a
job injury, the injury must happen at work (or a location
connected to work) and the injury must have been related to or
caused by the work. For instance, if someone gets the flu at
work and becomes ill, they are not covered for workers'
Compensation just because they got sick while at work.

The injury must be ACCIDENTAL (there are some specific exceptions
called occupational diseases). An accidental injury can be thought
of as an event a worker did not expect or plan to happen.
There must be an injury. An accident without a physical injury
may not in itself entitle the worker to any benefits.

Intentional injuries are not covered. If a worker is intoxicated
or on drugs AND THAT CAUSED THE INJURY they may not be covered.
Horseplay between employees is more often not covered than
covered. A worker is not covered on the way to and from work,

unless they are performing a special errand for the company on either of those trips. Workers are usually covered going from a company parking area to their job.

Workers who are assigned work out of town are covered as long as it is related to the job. When a worker is required to stay over-night out of town, most states recognize 24 hour coverage for injuries since the job requires them to be wherever they are.

Minors, illegal aliens, migrant workers are also usually covered unless the work category (i.e.: agriculture)is exempt in a particular area. There is no minimum or maximum age limit for coverage while on the job. Only workers are covered not their family members.

WHAT IS COVERED:

Basically any accidental injury on the job is covered.

It can range from a paper cut to being killed on the

job. The injury must not be pre-existing. There is an exception

for pre-existing injuries, in that if an accident makes the

condition worse, required treatments etc. are usually covered

until the person is as well as they were before the accident.

Normal sickness is not covered for the most part (one exception

might be medical staff that are surrounded by a particular disease

the public is not normally exposed to). A progression of the injury

is also covered provided it is related to the original injury.

As an example, a worker who developed blood toxins from a splinter

received on the job and later died, was covered at all stages for

the job injury. Mental problems are the most difficult to claim

and handle due to their nature, but they can also be covered under

certain circumstances such as a traumatic event or unexpected

situation that was so horrible as to cause a mental injury.

Conditions, which are not accidental injuries but can be directly

attributed to the workplace are sometimes covered depending on the

circumstances. Transport to a medical facility, hospital stay, tests, treatments, special trips to a facility are also usually

covered if the trips are directly related to a job injury.

Suicide is not covered for the most part although it has been covered in

some instances when it was proved that a supervisor or the job drove the

worker to suicide.

Radiation exposure may also be covered under specific circumstances but in

general occupational diseases or not covered under Workers' Compensation.

WHO PAYS FOR COVERAGE:

With very few exceptions, the employer pays 100% of the cost for the workers' compensation premium. In some rare circumstances such as a special contractor arrangement or a leasing program, the employee may be asked to pay for the cost of the workers' compensation premium if the employee would like to be covered. There is some legislation in discussion around the country which would require the employee to pay a portion or all of the workers' compensation premium cost, but at this time it is mostly in the discussion stage. Workers should not see any deductions for Workers' Compensation premiums unless they are in a special group. The cost of the Workers' Compensation premiums is usually built into the operating costs of the business. It is important to note that Workers' Compensation premium costs as well as claim costs have increased significantly over the years and are becoming a larger and larger burden for businesses and insurance carriers. There is a common confusion between Workers' Compensation and UNEMPLOYMENT COMPENSATION since they sound similar.

MEDICAL BENEFITS:

NOTE - ALL SPECIAL MEDICAL

PROCEDURES MUST BE APPROVED AND AUTHORIZED

BY THE TREATING PHYSICIAN AND MOST MUST HAVE

CARRIER APPROVAL IN ADVANCE OR THEY MAY

NOT BE COVERED!

DEDUCTIBLES:

Medical benefits for workers' compensation

injuries do not have a deductible amount before payment

or reimbursement is made. Medical bills related to the

job injury are paid in full according to the allowable

amount that can be charged. The amount that a doctor or

hospital can charge for a particular treatment comes from

a "fee schedule". Some special types of treatments are

exempt and the charge can be whatever is usual or customary.

These treatments have a special code number assignment.

The injured worker does not have to pay any difference in

what the fee schedule allows and what was actually billed.

15

Pharmacy charges are paid in full or reimbursed in full (if the injured worker paid for the medicine in advance), provided there is a prescription from the treating doctor. Lost wages have a type of deductible. In order to collect for lost time from work, most states require the worker to be unable to work for at least 7 calendar days (not work days). After the first seven days of being unable to work, the injured worker is entitled to lost time compensation. If the worker is out of work for more than 14 days (that is on the 15th day) the worker is paid for the first seven days of lost time from work. Of course, if the worker continues to receive salary, they are not entitled to any lost time compensation since there are no lost wages. Even though the worker is being paid salary while unable to work, the clock runs on the 7-14 day deductible as long as the worker is not working due to an accident. Sporadic lost workdays add up in a cumulative manner towards the 7 day criteria.

(Fee schedule and criteria can be obtained from the regulatory authority of a particular state).

COMMON EXAMPLES OF WORKERS' COMPENSATION BENEFITS

DEDUCTIBLE: None

LIMITS: None

CO-PAYMENT: None

REIMBURSEMENT: Yes

FEE SCHEDULE: Yes

PHARMACY: Yes

SPECIALISTS: Yes

NURSING HOME: Yes

HOME NURSE: Yes

MENTAL TREATMENTS/CONFINEMENTS: Yes

SURGERY: Yes

SPECIAL MEDICAL ITEMS: Yes

PLASTIC SURGERY: Yes

EXPERIMENTAL PROCEDURES: Yes (sometimes)

REHABILITATION COSTS: Yes (Is now required in some states)

LOST WAGE BENEFITS:

OF ALL WORKERS' COMPENSATION BENEFITS

THE LOST WAGE CALCULATION HAS THE

GREATEST VARIANCE FROM STATE TO STATE

CHECK THE RULES IN YOUR STATE.

COMMON CRITERIA SHOWN AS EXAMPLES

WAITING PERIOD: Yes, must be unable to work for a minimum time period

METHOD OF PAYMENT: Weekly until return to work

AMOUNT OF PAYMENT: Percentage of weekly salary (set maximum)

WEEKLY AMOUNT LIMIT: Yes maximum weekly and total amount set by law

TIME LIMIT FOR BENEFITS: Yes, with some exceptions

TIME LIMIT IN WEEKS: Yes on most cases, some exceptions

BENEFITS TAXED: No

PAYROLL DEDUCTIONS: No (standard deductions)

LOCATION PAID: Usually mailed directly to worker's home address

TERMINATION OF BENEFITS CRITERIA: Return to work, or able to return

MINIMUM WEEKLY AMOUNT: Yes, set by law

DISABILITY BENEFITS:

(COMMON EXAMPLES: CHECK YOUR STATE OR AREA)

PERMANENT DISABILITY BENEFITS: Yes

PARTIAL DISABILITY: Yes

TOTAL DISABILITY: Yes

LOSS OF USE OF (%): Yes

LOSS OF: Yes

AMOUNT: Based on schedule of body parts and weekly lost wage benefit

METHOD OF DETERMINATION OF DISABILITY: Doctor, AMA, Award by regulatory officer, visual inspection, tests and machines, rehabilitation expert.

PAYMENT TYPE: Lump sum, or weekly (depends on type and amount)

PAYMENT TO DEPENDENTS IF WORKER DIES WHILE RECEIVING
BENEFIT: Yes

PREEXISTING DISABILITY: Deducted from disability award (%)

PAYMENT FOR DISFIGUREMENT: Yes limited to a certain amount in
most states. The disfigurement must be visible in normal work attire, or
a burn scar or keloid (a raised scar). Some states may make exceptions for
women with regard to the visibility requirement.

NOTE: DISABILITY BENEFITS MAY BE COORDINATED WITH OTHER
BENEFITS IN MOST CASES AN INJURED WORKER CANNOT RECEIVE
DISFIGUREMENT AND DISABILITY FOR THE SAME INJURY.

Disability calculation method:

% Disability X Body part value (weeks) X Weekly Compensation Rate.

(As an example if total loss of the arm is 100 weeks, and the employee

has a disability rating of 10% they would be entitled to 100 X .10 or

10 weeks times their compensation rate).

NOTE: Regulatory authority may increase amount based on many

factors (age, education, type of work, etc.)

WAITING PERIOD:

Aside from the 7-14 day deductible in some states on lost

time compensation (lost wages), the insurance carrier

or the employer is allowed a certain amount of time to process

the claim before paying lost time compensation. It varies from

state to state but a rule of thumb is that the compensation must

start within 7-14 days from the date of the injury, or 7-14 days

from the date the worker started losing wages. In order for the

insurance company to comply, they must be notified by the employer

that the worker is on leave without pay. Some regulatory agencies

hold carriers liable for late payments of lost time compensation

even if the employer was late in notifying the carrier of the

injury. This is based on the rule that the employer (carrier)

must commence compensation within the required time so as not to cause the

employee hardship. There are penalties and fines for most instances of the

employer or insurance company not paying compensation as required by law.

The penalty usually goes to the injured worker in the form of a percentage of the

weekly benefit.

If any fine or penalty is the fault of the employer, the carrier

may refuse to pay and the employer may be held liable for those costs.

In general, most injured workers should have medical bills paid within 30 to 60 days and the worker should receive the first lost wage (lost time compensation) check within 2-3 weeks of the date of notice given to the employer by the injured worker. Claim denials or investigations greatly delay any benefits which are to be paid. Any amounts due at the time the first check is paid are included in the first check (Example: the worker has been out of work for 4 weeks and not paid. If the first lost wage compensation benefit check is sent in the 5th week, it includes the 5th week compensation due and the other 4 weeks due the worker for lost wage compensation due to the job injury).

REPORTING THE INJURY: IMMEDIATELY MEANS <u>WITHOUT DELAY</u>

1. Employees should be trained to report injuries IMMEDIATELY to their supervisor or proper official. The supervisor should report any employee injuries to proper channels within the company. IT IS CRITICAL that a business report injuries to the carrier IMMEDIATELY upon receiving notice of injury from the injured employee or other source. The carrier will need to respond to certain regulation requirements in order to prevent a fine against them or the workers' employer. The

carrier also needs to investigate doubtful claims before witness memories fade or they are influenced by other sources. Another important reason for immediately reporting the injury to the carrier is so the carrier can control medical costs and prevent costly treatments UP FRONT before they get out of control.

2. All injuries should be reported, no matter how minor they seem. If your state allows minor first aid injuries to NOT be reported, make sure you keep an internal record of the injury in case the information is later required for a multitude of reasons. Also you must make sure the injuries which you do not report qualify as NON-REPORTABLE injuries. THERE IS A DIFFERENCE INTERNALLY IN THAT EMPLOYEES SHOULD BE REQUIRED TO REPORT ALL INJURIES NO MATTER HOW MINOR!

3. Get the names of any witnesses to the injury or accident and keep a list. Interview witnesses as soon as possible and if important information is found, try to get a written statement. Keep asking "WHY" to every response until there is no possible answer to your question. Remember, a single claim no matter how minor, can end up costing MILLIONS in

medical and other benefits. It has happened!

4. Request all injury reporting and claims forms from the carrier if you do not already have them. If you have any questions, CALL THE CARRIER for help. Make sure the person filling out the forms knows what they are doing since any mistakes may be costly to both the company and the injured worker. It is not a good idea to let "just anyone" fill out injury forms. TRAIN THEM!

5. Fill out all forms IN FULL in writing and have the supervisor sign. You should also attach any important documents or records to THE HUMAN RESOURCE/SAFETY injury file on the injured worker.

6. Keep a copy of all completed forms for your records. Send copies of any information which you feel might help the carrier handle the claim, or defend a position taken on the claim.

7. Make sure all forms are signed and dated as required. Check

to make sure the dates and days are accurate in that the

date given is really the day given (example: Was February

8, really a Tuesday?). The times given on any form

must also match the actual work hours of the injured employee.

If key facts given by the injured worker do not match up

as they should, NOTIFY THE CARRIER.

8. Ask your carrier if they have any other suggestions.

TREATMENT FOR THE INJURED WORKER:

There are rules involving treatment for job injuries.

Failure to follow the rules of your state may result

in the bills being denied by the carrier.

Listed below are some common rules as examples.

These are possible suggestions for businesses if

they apply to your state:

1. Select a designated physician to treat injured workers.

This usually saves money and speeds the process.

2. A designated hospital should also be selected.

3. Make sure the injured employee tells the doctor the injury occurred

on the job.

4. Bills and treatment notes should be sent to the carrier.

The business may request copies also.

5. The injured worker should not go to another doctor unless referred by the treating physician (designated if possible).

6. The injured employee should seek emergency treatment (after physician office hours) in emergency only.

7. Make sure any doctor providing treatment handles Workers' Compensation cases.

8. Do not recognize "quack" doctors known to handle fraud claims as legitimate. Get the worker to another doctor ASAP!

9. Make sure the worker has a written prescription for any medications that have been requested to be paid. Watch out for narcotic abuse such an excessive use of a narcotic pain killer or other type of medication or drug.

10. If the worker is injured severely, request an ambulance. The cost of the ambulance may reduce the severity of the injury and the associated costs.

11.If the worker refuses medical treatment, DOCUMENT THE

REFUSAL and send a copy to the carrier ASAP.

12.Special procedures should be authorized in advance

by the carrier. The carrier may also offer alternative

treatments that may help the injured worker recover

faster from the injury at less cost.

EMERGENCY TREATMENT:

IN CASE OF EMERGENCY OR CRITICAL INJURY THE FOLLOWING ITEMS

MAY HELP THE INJURED WORKER AND REDUCE CLAIM COSTS:

1. Employees should call out someone is hurt. An employee should

be sent to notify the supervisor while others help the injured

worker. MAKE SURE OTHER EMPLOYEES ARE NOT IN A POSITION TO BE

INJURED ALSO.

2. Have someone call an ambulance for transport if the

injury is serious and moving the worker might cause

further injury. If in doubt, call the ambulance (911).

3. Make sure a qualified person administers first aid to control the injury to the worker and prevent further injury. IF IN DOUBT, DO NOT MOVE THE PERSON UNLESS THEIR LIFE IS IN DANGER FROM THE LOCATION.

4. Ask the injured worker what happened ASAP and get full details while the memory is fresh. Keep written notes.

5. If not obvious, ask if the injury happened on the job or if it was pre-existing.

6. Make sure all operating equipment is shut down as required in the immediate accident area so as to avoid any more employee injuries.

7. Don't let the injured worker continue to work if it might cause greater injury. Some injuries are worse than they look and continuing to work may cause a minor injury to turn into a critical injury. Internal injuries cannot be seen and some may be fatal. It is best to not take a chance and to send the injured

employee to a health care facility immediately unless it is totally obvious the injury is minor or not life threatening.

8. Notify family immediately if it is proper to do so.

9. Escort the worker to the treatment facility or have a representative go to the treatment facility to show you care about your employee!

10. Take the injured worker DIRECTLY to the hospital immediately (in case a blood test for a controlled substance is required due to condition of the worker).

11. Understand that the employee needs help promptly in order to get well and back to work. Delays can cost more than the initial treatments in the long run and increase your premiums.

12. Talk to witnesses as soon as possible to determine the cause of the accident and CORRECT THE CAUSE IMMEDIATELY to prevent another similar accident. Witnesses tend to forget details after periods of time or even change their story. Get a signed and dated witness statement.

13. Call your carrier if you need further instructions.

14. If there is a safety hazard which caused the accident, correct it before someone else gets hurt!

CHANGING DOCTORS:

BEFORE ALLOWING AN INJURED EMPLOYEE TO CHANGE DOCTORS TREATING THEM FOR A JOB INJURY, THESE GUIDELINES SHOULD BE EXAMINED AND FOLLOWED IF THEY APPLY IN YOUR STATE. IF YOU DO NOT FOLLOW PROPER PROCEDURES AND AUTHORIZE THE INJURED EMPLOYEE TO CHANGE DOCTORS, YOUR COMPANY MAY HAVE TO PAY THE BILL OR THE CLAIM MAY BE DENIED!

1. If the worker needs a specialist, the treating doctor must refer them.

2. Changing doctors without the permission of the carrier is not advised.

3. Changing doctors should only be allowed when absolutely necessary.

4. Make sure the new doctor accepts workers' compensation patients.

5. Be alert to "doctor shopping" by the worker for more time off.

6. Switching doctors too many times will result in worse treatment, not better.

7. Ask your carrier representative for the name of a doctor if you do not know one who handles workers' compensation injuries.

8. Try to avoid a personality problem with the treating doctor.

9. Before allowing the injured worker to change doctors, try to find out what the worker does not like about the treatment and discuss with the carrier.

10.Changing hospitals or rehabilitation persons is the same as doctors.

11.If the treating doctor seems to be "dragging out" the claim ask the carrier for a second medical opinion.

SPECIAL MEDICAL NEEDS RELATED TO THE INJURY:

For the most part any item or procedure which will tend to lessen the disability of the injured worker or limit the amount of time for recovery is usually authorized and paid for by the insurance carrier. The key is to have a prescription from the treating doctor for the item and to contact the insurance carrier in advance for approval.

Special medical items may include:

Wheelchairs, special beds, artificial limbs, home care, ramps, orthopedic shoes, contact lenses, and others.

All items must be related to the job injury in some way. Documentation from a reliable medical source is also usually required before special needs will be authorized and paid for by the carrier.

FAILURE TO OBTAIN ADVANCE AUTHORIZATION FROM THE CARRIER MAY RESULT IN CARRIER DENIAL OF THE BILL!

There are limits as to what procedures or equipment the carrier will authorize. As an example, some injured workers have obtained a medical prescription for a swimming pool at their home to help improve their injuries. As can be expected, carriers deny frivilous requests in most cases. Carriers may also deny doctor visits or treatments that were not authorized by the carrier or the treating physician.

PREEXISTING CONDITIONS:

As stated earlier in this book, an injury must be caused by the job in order for it to be considered workers' compensation. Conditions or medical problems that a person had prior to an accident are not covered for workers' compensation even if they first become evident on the job.

THERE IS ONE EXCEPTION TO THIS RULE. If an accident makes a pre-existing condition worse and it can be medically shown that is the case most states consider the worsening of the condition to be an accident. Of course the accident must still meet all of the other criteria to be workers' compensation. The accident must have happened at work, while working, and the work caused the accident and injury. Once a pre-existing condition is made worse by a job related accident the carrier is only responsible for making that person as well as they were before the job accident. If a person had a preexisting disability which was not made worse by the job accident, they would not get disability compensation. If it can be shown that a job injury increased a disability, the worker may receive the difference between the old and new disability in the form of a disability award and compensation. If the job injury totally disables an otherwise working person, the pre-existing condition deduction is not usually applicable.

INVESTIGATION:

Some injured workers or their employers may learn that the employer or carrier is investigating the job injury or workers' compensation claim.

There are many reasons why job injuries are investigated, they include:

1. The injury report is not complete.

2. Checking for safety problems or issues.

3. A routine audit of a certain percentage of claims.

4. A new employee with immediate accident.

5. A severe injury with associated high potential costs.

6. An employee history of large number of claims.

7. Conflicting accounts from the injured worker or witnesses of how the injury happened.

8. The accident happened immediately after a holiday or weekend.

9. A weekly compensation amount is unknown or the employee may have additional sources of income such as other jobs etc.

10. Suspicion of fraud.

11. Further information is needed to make decision to accept the claim.

12. Preparation for possible court action by worker or attorney.

13. Request by employer for carrier investigation.

Investigation is a key factor in reducing future accidents and the causes of those accidents. A reduction in the number of accidents or in the severity of accidents also reduces premium and other costs. The actual costs of the injury are minor compared to the other costs which are not directly related to any accident but increase due to the accident (lost productivity, employee overtime to make up for the loss of the injured worker, employee morale, employee loyalty, potential legal actions, staff time required to monitor or handle injury claim, etc.).

It has been suggested by many experts that the actual cost of the accident can be as little as 10-20% of the TOTAL costs of all matters related to the accident.

Investigation should begin internally IMMEDIATELY, to determine what went wrong and how to prevent another accident or injury. Share the results of the internal investigation with the insurance carrier since it may affect a decision to accept or deny a claim from their viewpoint. Internal investigations also help "trigger" an outside investigation by the carrier before benefits are paid on doubtful claims.

Make sure the person doing the investigation is trained in accident prevention and investigation, and that person is open minded enough to listen to ALL SIDES and not place blame on an individual when policies or systems may be at fault.

The forms provided in this publication are of a benefit in the investigation process and may help guide the investigator through the investigation process.

If YOUR CARRIER is investigating the accident, you should fully cooperate with them since they are trying to fix a problem that could prove very costly to a company, or find evidence to defend carrier denial of a workers' claim.

If another party is investigating the accident (Worker's attorney, OSHA, etc.) you may want to seek advice from the carrier or your attorney before providing too much information. OSHA (State or Federal Department of Labor) does have the authority to investigate accidents and conditions in many circumstances so in NO CASE should a company refuse to help OSHA (Department of Labor) unless they have been instructed to do so by LEGAL COUNSEL (Better get that in writing!). Since OSHA can fine companies large sums of money, caution is advised without legal advice since anything you say can and will be used against you (or so it seems to some

unfortunate companies). Whatever you do, do NOT lie to

investigators from any party, since that will only make matters

worse.

DENIAL OF CLAIM:

A very small percentage of workers' compensation claims actually get denied (10% or less in some states). The injured worker is notified of the denial of their claim by a letter from the insurance carrier or the employer. The majority of denied claims are denied from the beginning because they do not meet the requirements for a job related injury under the State laws. Another reason for claim denial is that the amount of injury exceeds the type of accident the worker had. A claim which is filed after the time period limit is almost always denied immediately pending investigation. Another time limit that causes denial is the reporting time requirement. If an accident is not immediately reported and there is not a good reason, the claim could be denied. Denial of the claim is not the end for the claim. A hearing can be requested from the regulatory authority for a review of the denial and the reasons. The regulatory authority has the right to order an insurance carrier or employer to accept the claim. Most carriers are reluctant to deny a claim without good reasons due to the associated legal costs to defend the denial. It has shown to be true that denying acceptable claims costs more in the long run than paying

them. Employer input is important as to whether a claim

is accepted or denied.

ATTORNEY FEES- (CHARGED TO THE INJURED WORKER):

Workers' compensation attorneys usually work on what is called a contingency fee, that is they do not get paid if they do not recover money for the injured worker on a claim. Most states have a limit as to the amount of money an attorney can charge an injured worker. Attorney fees charged to the worker are almost always subject to some type of approval by the Regulatory Authority (workers' compensation regulator).

A good rule of thumb on how much the worker will pay an attorney is:

No hearing or trial 10-33% of money paid on claim after expenses. (Some states may not allow the attorney to collect both a percentage and expenses for their time). Example attorney fees are based on a percentage of total compensation paid.

Settlement of claim without trial   33% of settlement AND expenses

Trial or hearing required   30-40% of total compensation paid AND

expenses

No money recovered   0

Expenses   Attorney hourly rate plus all expenses.

(Taken out of the injured worker's award in addition to the percentage charged or in some cases

Included in above percentages depending on State Laws.)

Rates may vary greatly depending on your state or area.

ATTORNEY FEES – (CARRIER OR EMPLOYER):

Of course the carrier must also hire an attorney in some cases.

These defense attorneys can charge from $100.00 to $ 500.00 per

hour for defending the claim for the carrier (and employer!).

The insurance carrier pays these attorney fees as part of policy holder/claim

services (unless the policy or agreement states otherwise). If the employer

engages an attorney the insurance company will almost always not pay for that

attorney.

HEARING PROCESS:

In workers' compensation, a review of a claim by an official
is called a hearing. Hearings have several uses: review of
denial; review of disability amount; complaints by worker about
lack of benefits; request for further treatment; request by the
carrier or employer to close the claim; determination of
dependents on a death claim (all death claims require a hearing
for this); request for an extension of benefits; request for a
fine against the carrier or employer; fraud hearing; and others.

TYPES OF HEARINGS:

1. Informal: Involves the carrier representative, employer, and worker.

2. Formal: Like a trial (attorneys, testimony, evidence).
A Notice of a Hearing is sent by the regulatory authority to the
worker, the employer, the insurance carrier, and any attorneys.
The notice includes the place and the time. The notice also states

what the issues are that will be handled at the hearing. Failure

to show at a hearing may result in the regulatory official ruling

against the party that did not show. It is not unusual for the hearing officer to

give the worker second chance if they do not show up. Businesses should make

sure a representative is present at any hearings involving the company or its

workers.

An issue may come up during testimony that may affect the outcome

of the hearing and input from the business representative may be

critical.

APPEALS:

The regulatory official does not have the last word on a

claims issue. Either the carrier or the worker may appeal

provided it is done in a timely manner (if the appeal is too

late, the appeal is rejected). The next step in some states for appeal of the

original ruling is a panel review of the original decision. The panel is composed

of several regulatory officials who did not hear the original issue.

From there the next step would be circuit court. Circuit court

reviews the legal issues and whether the laws were applied

properly by the hearing officials. If an attorney does not bring up an

issue in the appeal request or earlier hearings, those issues are

usually not heard by the court. The next step would be the Court

of Appeals or the State Supreme Court. To appeal a claim to these

levels can take years and cost large sums of money for the carrier.

Once the Supreme Court rules on an issue, that ruling becomes

Law and applies to all claims until another ruling changes

the ruling on the issue. Attorneys are required on both sides for most appeals

especially those involving the court system.

TIME FRAMES FOR ACTIONS (SOME COMMON EXAMPLES):

1. Compensation check sent   14-30 days from notice of accident

2. Medical bill payment   14-90 days from billing

3. Disability rating   Upon maximum healing of injury

4. Disability award lump sum   14-30 days after rating approved

5. Appeal of hearing   6-12 months after request

6. Appeal to court   6 months to 1 year

7. Supreme Court appeal   1-5 years

8. Acceptance of claim   1-30 days

9. Denial of claim   1-30 days

10. Carrier review   2 weeks - 6 months (denial review)

(Includes Investigation)

11. Reporting Injury   IMMEDIATELY, 10-14 days for business,

                                        Immediately to 90 days for employee.

                                        There is also a statute of limitations.

                                        (see #12 below)

12. Filing a claim   Immediately to state law: time limit.

                                        (Example: 2 years in SC) Failure to

                                        file a claim in time is a strong

                                        denial for carriers and businesses and

                                        may deny the claim or benefits FOREVER.

REVERSAL OF DECISION:

No matter which decision was made on a claim, it can be reversed by the regulatory officials or the court system. The problem begins if money has been paid to the injured worker. There are some provisions which allow the insurance carrier or the employer the right to ask for the money back from the worker. This is especially true when it comes to claims which are declared to be fraudulent. If the insurance carrier is allowed to deny a previously accepted claim, the doctor's office or hospital is notified of the denial and money received is refunded to the insurance carrier. The injured worker is then billed for services and they may use health insurance if it is available. If the worker does not have health insurance, they may have to pay for the medical treatments.

Most health insurance carriers will NOT pay a suspected job injury until they receive an official letter of denial from the workers' compensation carrier and even then they may fight the issue. If the claim was originally denied as workers' compensation and then accepted, the health insurance carrier is notified and the workers' compensation carrier pays the group health carrier direct for any bills they paid on the work injury if it was handled as a group health claim. The worker is also reimbursed for any deductibles or co-payments they made under health insurance requirements.

REASONS FOR DENIAL:

THERE ARE AN INFINITE NUMBER OF REASONS WHY CLAIMS ARE DENIED SINCE THE DECISIONS ARE USUALLY MADE BASED ON THE JUDGMENT OF INSURANCE CARRIER EMPLOYEES. LISTED BELOW ARE EXAMPLES OF COMMON REASONS FOR DENIALS.

1. No coverage by the carrier because of non payment of premiums, violation of insurance policy requirements, or failure of the employer to provide proper information on the claim.

2. Accident happened while not working on the job.

3. Medical records do not support the accident claim.

4. Investigation revealed conflicting facts on claim.

5. Claim form has conflicting information.

6. Important information is missing from claim form.

7. Employer has requested denial by the carrier.

8. Reporting of injury is late (grace period varies) which results in automatic denial pending investigation.

9. Medical records state medical condition was present before the accident.

10. Details of the accident don't make sense (not logical).

11. Medical condition is not job related (normal disease i.e.: Flu etc.).

12. Witnesses state they did not see any injury or accident as claimed.

13. Acceptance is not allowed under state law (most common reason).

FRAUD:

Fraud (filing false claims mostly for money or payment of medical bills not from a job injury) costs everyone in one way or another. Fraud has increased over recent years according to most available information. One negative result of fraud is that it slows the payments to legitimate injuries since the insurance carrier or employer has to investigate more and more claims to make sure they are legitimate. Fraud also costs money in that the more claims payments that are made, the higher the premium that must be charged. If a company has to pay more for higher premiums, they may have to lay-off employees or give a smaller raise to employees.

Fraud is also committed by companies in the premium calculation process. Some companies give false payroll figures to the insurance carriers and give false job descriptions in order to reduce the premium (lower the risk, lower the premium). Business fraud costs other businesses through higher rates. Fraud is ILLEGAL and is punishable by fines and prison terms in most states in one form or another. If the insurance carrier determines you have misled them, they will perform and audit and charge you the proper amount for up to three years total or may deny any and call claims.

IF YOU THINK SOMEONE IS COMMITTING FRAUD, CALL THE CARRIER AND ASK THEM FOR INSTRUCTIONS ON HOW TO HANDLE THE SITUATION.

SOME THINGS INJURED WORKERS MIGHT ATTEMPT:(FRAUD)

Be alert to these possibilities and notify the carrier

if you suspect any of these.

1. Presenting misinformation about the injury or accident.

2. Falsify records.

3. Not filling out injury form completely (avoiding information

which might result in non-acceptance of the claim) in order to hide details of the

injury or accident.

4. Giving wrong or different times or dates for the injury (common when

injury DID NOT actually happen).

5. Telling co-workers they are going to get even with the company.

6. Threatening the person handling the claim.

7. Trying to get the carrier to pay for things not related to a

job injury.

8. Filing one silly claim after another.

9. Using a false name or maiden name after marriage.

10.Trying to get the doctor to give a high disability rating for more money or "doctor shopping".

11.Going to an attorney the same day they report an accident.

12.Finding a doctor who is known to help fraudulent claims filing.

13.Not asking permission from the carrier or employer for a change of some kind.

14.REFUSING MEDICAL TREATMENT!

15.Faking an injury soon after finding out they are going to be the target of lay-offs or termination.

WAYS TO RECOGNIZE POSSIBLE EMPLOYEE CLAIM FRAUD:

Be alert to these possibilities and notify the carrier

if you suspect any of these.

1. Waiting until the next workday to fake an accident in

order to make it appear an injury that occurred away from

work is work related. This is done for no medical deductible

and disability compensation if accepted instead of

the usual benefits if filed through the group health plan.

In addition to the medical benefits an accepted fraud

claim results in the injured person collecting lost

wages and permanent disability benefits which they would

not collect if the injury was not accepted as a job

injury.

2. Getting an agreement from other worker(s) to be a

"witness" to an accident which did not occur, and

paying the "witness" after disability is collected.

3. Putting multiple body parts injured on the claim form

in order to try and collect more money from a disability

rating and make the accident appear more serious than

it really was.

4. Claiming a fake psychological injury in addition to physical

injury in order to make the issue more complicated

and attempt to collect total disability from a minor

accident. Due to the high costs of mental treatments,

this may encourage settlement by the carrier on doubtful

claims.

5. Sharing ways to collect money and commit fraud with co-workers.

6. Not following company policy after a work injury and then

threatening to sue for retaliatory discharge. Some states permit

workers to sue and collect if they can prove the employer

discharged them for filing a claim or if the employer takes action

against the worker for not following policy. A type of

"blackmail".

7. Filing for every type of insurance or disability benefits

available (social security, long term disability, etc.)

and trying to collect all benefits at once by not telling

carriers about a workers' compensation injury, or vice-versa.

8. Repeated injuries in an attempt to finally get some money on

one or more injuries. Be alert to this.

9. Using multiple social security numbers to hide other job

injuries, and using different names including deceased

person's names.

10.Using out-of-state doctor for disability rating so it is more

difficult to check the accuracy of the rating and the

credentials of the doctor.

11.Working as self employed while drawing compensation benefits.

12.Claiming multiple accidents with multiple employers.

13.Collecting benefits while in jail (YES! It happens more than you

would like to believe.)

14. Intentionally hurting themselves in order to collect money.

15. Deliberate re-injuring of the injury to make the disability period longer and attempt to collect more permanent disability.

16. Attempts to report a job injury as the cause of alcohol or drug addiction problems.

17. If an injury looks "funny" or strange investigate fully or hire an outside accident investigator if needed. The fraudulent worker usually does not realize how silly a fraud claim looks. Be alert to "funny" looking claims.

18. Trying to collect from workers' compensation on an old military or other (football etc.) injury by faking a new accident.

19. Faking doctor's prescriptions (especially when the injured worker is a drug addict) and excuses, and in some cases disability ratings.

20. Having a family member or friend impersonate a home health care

worker and bill for services in order to collect money for that in addition to other benefits.

21.Family members will sometimes "FAKE" that an injured worker is still alive (in cases of injured worker death due to a cause unrelated to the job injury such as murdered, drugs, auto accident, Etc.) in order to continue receiving and cashing the compensation checks.

22.Selling prescription narcotics, received due to the job injury, to people on the street for cash.

22.ANY OF THESE MAY RESULT IN AN ORDEER BY THE REGULATORY AUTHORIT FOR REPAYMENT OF FUNDS RECEIVED BY THE FRAUDULANT PERSON TO THE CARRIER\COMPANY, OR IN SOME CASES PRISON TERMS. MANY STATES HAVE OR ARE CONSIDERING FRAUD LAWS AND INVESTIGATION RIGHTS BY STATE GOVERNMENT WHEN FRAUD IS SUSPECTED ON WORKERS' COMPENSATION CLAIMS. REPORT SUSPECTED FRAUD TO THE CARRIER IMMEDIATELY.

TYPES OF WORKERS' COMPENSATION INSURANCE CARRIERS:

The term CARRIER is another way of saying the company that provides the workers' compensation coverage, since the insurance company "carries" the risk and benefits payable on behalf of the employer.

There are several types of carriers or providers for workers' compensation coverage. All carriers must be registered with the agency which regulates workers' compensation. Most carriers are also required to meet financial and reporting requirements according to the State department of insurance regulations.

SOME MAIN AND COMMON CARRIER TYPES:

1. Private insurance company

2. State Compensation Fund

3. Assigned Risk Pool

4. Association Pool

5. Self-Insurance Pool

6. Employer Self Insurance (the employer assumes the risk).

7. Service Carrier (handles claims for other companies. Assumes

no risk or financial responsibility). Not really a carrier,

but some carriers provide this special service to self

insured businesses or pools.

8. Reinsurance Carrier (provides reinsurance for excess losses).

Reinsurance pays when the level of losses for a particular

period exceeds a predetermined policy level. Some carriers

provide reinsurance, some carriers specialize in reinsurance. All

Self-insured businesses or pools should have reinsurance.

ALTERNATE PROGRAMS TO WORKERS' COMPENSATION:

As the costs of workers' compensation coverage grow, so do proposed cost saving programs as alternatives to traditional coverage. These change daily, but the most common being discussed are:

1. Replacing workers' compensation with a liability type of coverage.

2. Employee leasing programs.

3. Workers' compensation coverage would be optional for employers and replaced by some other form of accident coverage insurance.
(OPTING OUT – Not allowed in most states)

4. Allow the employee to sue the employer for job injuries.

5. Require the employee to pay a portion of the coverage cost.

6. Require the employee to pay a deductible amount for job injuries.

7. State programs to pay claims of bankrupt companies

(Self-insured companies or businesses).

8. 24 Hour combined health and accident coverage.

(Covers employees whether at work or not)

9. Federal workers' compensation program to replace state

programs. This is part of proposed National Health

Care plans.

10.Require employers to have safety programs to prevent accidents.

There is general doubt as to whether changing the current systems

will help or hurt businesses and employees. Cost savings are still

being tracked on some of the newer alternatives and results are

unknown at this time.

The general rule for alternate programs is to make sure that any company is

established and reputable and they can support any alleged savings with facts

and figures. The most important thing to remember is BUYER BEWARE. The

worst thing that could happen to any business is to have a large workers' compensation claim and their insurance carrier not support or protect the business as they said they would. It is for that reason that any policy be READ entirely before accepting the coverage for the business, especially on new or alternate programs.

It is important to check for many aspects of an alternative program, including self-insurance. Primarily the most important thing to remember is that the financial position of a business must be protected against excessive losses of any kinds including JOB INJURIES. Make sure any alternative program does not violate any law (the business will be held responsible) and can be depended on to pay benefits due an injured employee no matter how much that injury may cost (some work injuries can cost over a million dollars!). It is also important to select reinsurance from a financially stable and reputable company that will be able to pay any large amounts due on excessive loss claims. Leasing programs are like anything else in that the company chosen must be of quality and reputable. Make sure the leasing company does provide Workers' Compensation coverage and can PROVE IT with a certification letter of coverage from a reputable

insurance carrier or program. Trying to "bypass" workers'

compensation rules by leasing is not only a bad decision,

it is also dangerous to the business financially and

could result in serious legal problems. Get anything in

writing and READ THE CONTRACT CAREFULLY. It is also a good

idea to a have an attorney who is an EXPERT in workers'

compensation look at the contract and point out possible

problem areas.

Alternatives may or may not work. The thing to remember is that

you can do something NOW to reduce your costs. If you do not

take actions to reduce costs, no program can save you money.

Once out of the voluntary workers' compensation insurance

market, it may not be easy to obtain workers' compensation

coverage at a later date especially if nothing was done to

reduce job injuries or costs.

EMPLOYEE LEASING: SOME KEY POINTS

MOST COMMON POINTS

1. Regulated by the State regulatory authority

2. Rules developed by the NCCI (In most areas

or other similar rate making/statistical

organization).

IMPORTANT QUESTIONS TO ASK AND POINTS TO LOOK FOR

WHEN CONSIDERING AN EMPLOYEE LEASING PROGRAM:

1. Does the employee leasing firm have an approved

carrier who provides coverage for ALL of their

employees, including those leased? If the carrier

is not approved by the regulatory authority, you

may be in trouble if you have a claim.

2. Do employees of the leasing firm meet the

employee/employer test (this determines who is liable

for injuries) under state rules? If they do not,

any agreement with the leasing firm may be overturned

by the regulatory authority or court system.

3. What happens if the leasing firm denies coverage on

a "leased" employee, or denies the claim? Are you left

with the bills and fines? If so, look out.

4. If a business is determined to be an "unqualified self

insurer" the regulator may be able to fine a business

for every day the business did not have coverage.

These fines can be VERY EXPENSIVE.

5. Does the leasing firm have a valid certificate of insurance

from a state APPROVED carrier? Has certificate been

verified as authentic? Fake certificates or canceled

coverage is not unheard of. If the leasing company does not

have valid coverage YOU must pay for the claim.

6. In some states a carrier may not be allowed to provide coverage

other than to actual employees of the leasing company. Does

this rule apply in your state? If this rule does apply in your state you may still be liable for losses and may not have coverage!

7. Do other employees of the leasing firm have high or low

claim losses? Don't water down a group of bad losses

with your good loss record. You don't need to subsidize

other high risk companies with your low claims and good safety record.

8. Would your own experience rating be lower than the rating

of the leasing firm? You may not be saving anything and may

be paying more if the answer is YES.

9. Some regulators may be of the opinion that under common law,

the worker is an employee of the company where they are

actually doing the work. How does this affect leasing

agreement? Does leasing company have an "all states"

endorsement on the workers' compensation policy? It could

be a problem is an employee is injured in another state

and files for benefits in that state, and the leasing

firm or carrier will only pay benefits from the state

in which they are located (a serious problem if the outside

state has higher benefits than the leasing location

state).

10. Is there a written guarantee on the part of the leasing firm that they will be liable for all injuries of workers leased through them? Are ALL claims costs paid by the leasing firm or their carrier? Legal costs? In some cases, the actual amount paid on a claim can be far less than the associated costs of a denied claim, or a problem claim.

11. Has the relationship of liability coverage for the business and the leasing plan been discussed with the liability carrier? Is there some type of employer's liability coverage and, who is responsible? Check with your liability carrier if you retain liability and verify the affect leasing might have on liability coverage.

12. Is the leasing firm changing name each year to avoid NCCI experience rating of employees? If so, this is not good.

13. Has the leasing arrangement been reviewed and approved by the attorney for the business leasing the employees? Not a bad

idea to have an attorney look over any arrangement.

14.Is there documentation to prove the employees of the leasing firm are being recorded and handled as such (Federal and State laws, IRS, Tax Commission, Health Plan, FICA, etc.) Try to get proof or copies of relevant documents.

15.Who writes payroll checks? This may determine who is liable for injuries on contested claims.

16.If the leasing firm is just a payroll company who doesn't hire or fire, you should BE CAREFUL in using their plan.

17.Is leasing firm self-insured? Is the self-insurance financially solvent? Try to obtain verifiable proof of solvency and compliance with state self-insurance rules.

18.Does the leasing firm have separate policies for each client who is covered in the assigned risk pool? If not, be careful.

19.Is the leasing firm FULL SERVICE?:

Employee benefits

Cobra

Workers' Compensation

Safety

Discounts

Payroll

RISA plans

Retirement.

20.Is the leasing company a member of a

NATIONAL LEASING ASSOCIATION? Being

a member of a national association is a plus, if they

are not a member why not?

EXEMPT EMPLOYEES: These employees are usually NOT covered under Worker's Compensation Laws.

1. Casual employees – Pick up labor

2. Agriculture and Rail

3. Volunteers (some)

4. Requested exemption

5. Independent Contractor – Totally independent (you have no control over their actions and they use their own equipment).

6. Employees who work on shipping lanes (Longshoreman's act coverage). This also applies to any employees who work on waters used by shipping navigation. This is a special coverage and is under Federal law.

7. Federal military

8. CHECK YOUR STATE RULES (Obtain from state regulatory agency)

REGULATORY AUTHORITIES:

Regulatory authorities exist to make sure the workers'
Compensation system flows as intended by state law. The
regulatory agency is a state agency with powers to order
specific actions on workers' compensation claims. Most top officials
of regulatory agencies are appointed by the legislature or the
Governor of the state. Some states require the hearing officers
to be attorneys, some do not.

Regulatory agencies go by many names a few common examples are;
Industrial Commission; Workers' Compensation Commission; Employee
Accident Board; State Accident Board; State Department of Insurance;
and others. The hearing officials are referred to as hearing
officers, commissioners, judges, review board members, and
other terms. Regulatory authorities usually have the right to
issue a subpoena, a bench order, or fine. They also have the
right to order a worker to pay back money received on a claim.
Most criminal actions are turned over to a State Law Enforcement
Agency for handling. The regulatory authority also provides
information to anyone who needs it, and collects statistical

information.

TIPS FOR FASTER CLAIM HANDLING:

1. <u>DO NOT DELAY IN REPORTING THE ACCIDENT TO THE CARRIER</u>. Fill out and/or send the forms IMMEDIATELY once you have been notified of an accident or injury. Make sure the injury report or claim form is filled out in full, signed, and dated. Forms are usually sent to the carrier.

Note: In some states small "medical only" claims are not required to be reported to the carrier or the regulatory officials but YOU MUST KEEP AN INTERNAL RECORD of the accident.

The carrier forwards all required information to the regulatory agency. Businesses should keep COPIES of all information sent to carriers and the date each was sent. Check with your carrier to determine which types of claims do not have to be reported. No matter what, the employee should report all injuries AND A RECORD KEPT by the business internally.

2. Be specific on accident and injury details. Do not leave out facts that may be useful in handling of the claim. Take

81

time to ask questions carefully and verify the information

before sending the first report of injury to the carrier or

regulatory authority. If you do not have detailed information,

ask witnesses, the injured worker, and any other person

who can give specific details regarding the accident or

injury. Remember, there are restrictions on the time allowed

to report an injury.

3. The day, the date, and time of the accident must be

accurate. If these do not match, it may result in a delay

due to carrier investigation or denial.

4. Report the accident immediately (if required) even if it is a

minor injury. First aid injuries may not have to be reported

in your state. If not required, you must still keep

detailed and accurate records of the minor injury in case

further medical treatment is required. If you are

required to send in a formal report at a later date,

BE SURE TO INCLUDE A LETTER TO THE REGULATORY AUTHORITY

stating the injury was initially handled as a minor

non-reportable first aid only case. If you do not include

that information, you may be subject to a fine.

5. Make sure the injured employee tells all doctors etc. the condition is from a job injury. Employee should be instructed to be totally honest with the treating physician and not try to hold back any information. If the employee's information to the doctor is not accurate or appears to be misleading, the claim may be investigated or denied by the carrier. This will delay the handling of the claim. Carriers are entitled to ALL medical treatment records including notes!

6. Ask the carrier for permission or guidance before authorizing the injured worker to change doctors etc., if a business does not ask permission from the carrier and authorizes treatment, the carrier may deny the charges and the business may have to pay for the costs of the treatment after a hearing is held on the matter. Any problems can be avoided up front by contacting the carrier in advance.

7. Make sure the carrier knows if the injured employee is being paid salary while out due to a job injury.

AVOID overpayment of compensation! Check the salary

used to calculate the compensation rate. Make sure the

correct amount is used by both the reporting business and the

carrier when calculating the compensation rate. If it

appears the injured worker is not losing pay due to the

job injury, compensation benefits will not be started by

the carrier. If the carrier is unaware the worker has

returned to work, payments of compensation benefits may

continue. It may be difficult, and in some cases impossible,

for the carrier or business to recover overpayments of

compensation. These mistakes increase premiums.

8. Complete all forms that are requested from the carrier

quickly and in full being as accurate as possible. Without

the proper forms completed as needed, the carrier cannot

do their job properly or timely. If proper information is

not received, the carrier may suspend or terminate benefits

as allowed by law. This causes problems and usually leads

to attorney involvement.

9. Keep copies of all information about the job injury. Due to

ADA rules, it is not suggested that the injury information be kept in the same file as personnel information.

10.Keep receipts of anything paid in cash related to the injury, both by the business and the injured worker. In most instances, both can be reimbursed for related expenses. Having receipts will definitely speed up the reimbursement process.

11.Request detailed mileage records for reimbursement requests for trips to the doctor by the employee. Check accuracy before sending any request for reimbursement to the carrier. Check the miles listed to see if they represent the actual distance (map miles). Also check the dates of doctor visits on the bills, with the dates listed for mileage reimbursement for trips to the doctor. Usually the trip to the doctor must be farther than an certain distance (10 miles as an example) to qualify for reimbursement.

12.Know the name and phone number of the person handling

your worker's claim, and work with them. They are on your

side. Do not take the attitude "that's their job at the

Insurance carrier" unless you do not care that it is "your money"

being spent and it will be reflected in your next premium.

13.Check on anything you think is late (check with the carrier

representative or doctor). It is important to follow up on the

claim progress to make sure things are going smoothly.

A little time spent here can help prevent a lot of

headaches down the road for everyone.

14.Notify carrier if the injured worker changes address or phone

number. It is best to notify the carrier of any change which

occurs while the claim is still open (including marriage,

marital status, dependents, etc.).

15.Supply requested information immediately to carrier when requested.

16.If your carrier cannot obtain information, try to assist

them (ex. doctor reports). Remember, claims costs affect your

company also. If you have to, go to the doctor to obtain the medical records

clerk in person or see the doctor. If the insurance carrier

sends someone to obtain required information it may cost you

extra in the claims handling since all expenses are basically billed

back to the claim.

The faster a claim is handled properly and accurately, the less cost to

all parties.

DEATH CLAIMS:

Death on the job does not seem to fit in with the concept
of helping the injured worker. In recognition of the loss
of income due to a job injury, there is a death benefit for
the surviving dependents of the worker. Most states use
the term "spouse" which means the husband or wife is entitled
to survivor benefits. Children are also protected, in that
there are usually provisions which specify how much of the death
benefits will go directly to the children. If the child or
children are minors, a guardian is usually appointed to look after
their interests. Biological children from non-married couples
are also considered dependents for purposes of benefits
(If either biological parent is killed on the job). If a
Legally separated spouse is killed on the job, the estranged
husband or wife may not be entitled to any benefits if
they were living apart. If there is no spouse or child,
benefits are sometimes paid to another dependent or parents.
In some cases with no qualified dependents, the benefits
are paid to the state (Second Injury Fund).

Death benefit amounts are usually the same as total

disability benefits, but are paid as a lump sum in most cases.

The same limits usually apply to death claims as in total

disability, including maximum compensation rates and the

total number of weeks paid.

ALL DEATH CLAIMS ARE INVESTIGATED FOR THE FOLLOWING REASONS:

If the insurance carrier or business does not locate a dependent

child or other, and the benefit is paid to a party or parties,

the dependent, which was not located or known, can come back

at a later date and the carrier or business WILL HAVE TO PAY

THEM ALSO which means benefits paid were not properly divided

and the amount paid was more than necessary (a type of "double

payment"). That is why carriers and businesses investigate death

claims in full.

OSHA also is involved in some death cases and is another

reason for investigations. Death claims are investigated to determine who was dependent, ages of dependents, who qualifies for benefits,

number of children, previous marriages, marital status,

cause of death (work related or not), and to gain information

to complete death claim forms mailed to the regulatory officials.

INVESTIGATION OF A DEATH CLAIM IS NOT UNUSUAL AND SHOULD NOT

BE TAKEN AS A SIGN THE INSURANCE CARRIER OR BUSINESS IS

GOING TO DENY THE CLAIM!

Everyone should cooperate with the investigation including honest answers to

some pretty tough and personal questions (such as are there any children

by anyone else other than the wife, etc.). The questions

must be asked, so no one should be offended or take it as

a personal attack on a person's character. Some states

may differ on death claims, but the general rule regarding

the rights of dependents may apply in a large number of states.

If a business knows of dependents other than those commonly

known or already discovered by the carrier, the business

should notify the carrier IMMEDIATELY so the matter can

be investigated and "double payment" avoided.

When an employee is fatally injured on the job, the business

has a moral responsibility to do everything possible to help

the family of the deceased employee obtain benefits they

are LEGITIMATELY entitled to.

It is unfortunate that fatal claims can be less expensive than

Total disability claims because the medical costs are usually

minimal and the amount of total compensation is known from the

start. This is in contrast to a long time claim with

extensive medical bills and compensation with no definite

conclusion date.

BUSINESS COVERAGE REQUIREMENTS:

Workers' Compensation coverage is available in one form or another to all businesses who are required to have workers' compensation coverage for employees.

Laws mandate coverage if a business meets certain requirements. One example would be the number of employees. In some cases, such as public employees, coverage is required with no exceptions. Failure to provide coverage as required, may result in penalties ranging from fines to prison terms. Companies who do NOT have Workers' Compensation coverage may also be liable for civil action by injured employees. Civil actions related to job injuries are NOT covered in most cases by the liability coverage of the business. Some businesses that did not have workers' compensation coverage have been forced to liquidate in order to pay for large legal judgments resulting from employee job injuries and lack of coverage.

Employers' liability coverage is now an important part of Workers' Compensation, as injured employees continue to take job injuries to Court for civil action and additional benefits. If a job injury results in a judgment beyond the Workers' Compensation coverage

limits of a policy, the remainder of the judgment would be paid

by the business if the business did NOT have employer's liability

coverage. The Workers' Compensation carrier will only pay the

amount that the policy covers (benefits set by law for Workers'

Compensation injuries). Employers are advised to consider

purchasing employer's liability if they have not already done

so. THIS IS IN ADDITION TO STANDARD WORKERS' COMPENSATION

COVERAGE. The larger the coverage amount limits purchased, the

better!

JOB INJURY POLICY EXAMPLES (INTERNAL):

Check your state for regulations or requirements.

Notice to employees: This job injury policy is for your protection and must be followed if you are injured on the job. Failure to follow proper procedures may delay benefits or result in claim denial by the Insurance carrier. Please fill in all forms entirely, making sure all information is accurate.

Your company wants all employees to have a safe working environment. It is also the intent of your company to provide all required information to the Workers' Compensation Insurance Carrier in order to expedite any benefits due an injured employee.

1. REPORTING PROCEDURES:

Any employee who is injured on the job is required to take the following steps:

1. Take any action possible to reduce the injury (example: if substance is in eyes, flush eyes by using eyewash station) by applying

first aid treatment if applicable. The injured employee should NOT

continue working if they feel they have seriously injured themself.

2. Notify the immediate supervisor immediately. "Immediately" is

defined as the moment the employee knows they have had an accident

and/or injured them self. If the direct supervisor is not available,

notify an appropriate supervisor or official.

3. Fill out in full, the following forms:

A. Company job injury report form

B. Detailed job injury report form (if requested)

C. Safety report

4. If required, or instructed by supervisor, the employee should

seek immediate treatment from the company-designated physician.

The designated physician name and location will be supplied to all

employees. The use of a designated physician can speed treatment to

injured employees.

5. If emergency, the employee should seek immediate treatment from

the designated emergency treatment facility.

2. SEEKING TREATMENT

When seeking treatment for an injury which occurred on the job, the injured employee must follow these procedures:

1. Seek treatment from the designated physician for the company, sometimes called "the company doctor".

2. Seek treatment from the designated emergency treatment facility of the company (if emergency). If released from the emergency facility, the employee must seek additional treatment from the designated company physician. Do not return to the emergency facility unless it is a true emergency and cannot wait until the designated physician can be seen during normal business hours.

3. Notify all treating physicians that the injury is job related and GIVE FULL DETAILS on how the accident happened.

4. Ask the treating physician or facility to file with the Workers' Compensation carrier of the company.

5. Keep any appointment, do not miss any appointments without a valid reason.

6. Do not change physicians without a referral by the designated physician. Changing without permission from the designated physician or the insurance carrier may result in denial of payment for the unauthorized treatments!

7. The injured employee must provide the company with a written excuse from the designated physician for time off.

8. In the event the designated physician is not providing proper treatment, the injured employee must request authorization to change physicians from the Workers' Compensation Insurance Carrier. The Insurance carrier may give the injured employee the name of another physician for further treatment.

9. If there is lost time from work due to the job injury, and the

designated physician releases the injured employee to return to work, the employee must report to work on the day authorized by the physician.

10. Reimbursement for amounts paid relating to the job injury by the injured worker should be requested from the insurance carrier. Written, itemized, and official statements will be required by the Insurance carrier for any reimbursements to the injured worker. The injured employee should seek authorization prior to paying for treatment or items, in order to make sure the insurance carrier will reimburse for the costs paid by the injured worker. It is important to note that treatments, drugs, and other items should be billed directly to the insurance carrier for the best handling of the charges unless instructed otherwise. If a business or facility does not handle Workers' Compensation claims, contact the insurance carrier for the names of businesses who will.

3. ACCIDENT PREVENTION AND SAFETY

In addition to the reporting and treatment requirements, it is the responsibility of ALL employees of the company to make sure accidents are prevented whenever possible.

1. Injured employees are expected to tell the supervisor what caused the accident so the situation can be corrected immediately in order that no one else is injured the same way.

2. Employees who are injured on the job should never try to "hide" the details of the accident. The purpose of accident prevention is not to place blame, but rather to make sure employees have a safe working environment. An accident is an accident. There is no such thing as a "stupid" accident. Employees should feel free to report any accidents and provide clear and exact details of:

A. What lead up to the accident?

B. How the accident happened

C. How the accident could have been prevented

D. Any violations of safety rules by others that caused the accident.

3. Employees who do not use proper safety devices or follow proper safety procedures cannot be denied Workers' Compensation benefits for job injuries, however the employee who fails to follow proper policies

or procedures may be subject to disciplinary action or termination based on our safety policy and safety rules or a reduction in benefits.

4. LOST TIME DUE TO JOB INJURY

In order to collect any benefits for time lost from work due to a job injury, the employee must meet certain requirements of the Insurance carrier. These requirements include but are not limited to:

1. Treating physician (designated physician) written excuse for time off from work, with reason, dates, times, and other important information including WHETHER OR NOT THE CONDITION IS JOB RELATED.

2. The time off from work must be directly related to the job injury.

3. A written excuse must be provided to the company on a weekly basis unless the appropriate company official allows a less frequent schedule for written excuses (in cases where the injury is severe and it is obvious the injured employee will be unable to work for a long period of time). The company has the right to require a weekly excuse for lost

time from work (per employee handbook) but may change the requirement

at the discretion of the company, in certain instances where the weekly

excuse requirement would cause undue hardship on the injured employee

or the company. The company will notify the injured employee in writing

if the decision is made to waive the weekly excuse requirement.

4. If the company waives the weekly excuse requirement for an employee

injured on the job, the employee will be required to submit a written

excuse upon request by the company, within one week of the request.

The company reserves the right to request a written excuse from the

treating (designated) physician at any time. The company also has

the right to request the injured worker see the treating physician

if the company (or carrier) needs more information.

5. The insurance carrier or the company may request any information

required by company policy or Workers' Compensation rules or law.

Failure to submit the requested information in a timely manner may

result in a suspension of benefits by the insurance carrier and/or

a request by the insurance carrier to the Workers' Compensation

Authority to terminate the benefits. If the failure to submit

requested information violates the employee policy rules of the

101

company, the injured employee who violates the policy may be subject to disciplinary action or termination.

6. Injured employees who are unable to work, and are receiving lost time benefits for a job related injury, and work at another job while receiving lost time benefits, may be required to pay the insurance carrier back for the benefits received for lost time paid during the period. Legal action for FRAUD may also be possible.

7. Lost time benefits to injured employees are the responsibility of the Workers' Compensation Insurance Carrier and not the company. Employees who are unable to work due to a job injury, are placed on leave of absence without pay. Lost time benefit checks will come from the Workers' Compensation Insurance Carrier on a weekly basis. Benefit checks are usually mailed directly to the injured employee at their home address. Failure to provide a current and proper address may result in the injured employee not receiving timely benefits.

8. Injured employees must be unable to work for a period of time (days) before they are entitled to lost time benefits due to a job injury. In order to ease the burden on the injured employee, the

company may allow the injured employee to use paid leave for days

lost from work during the first days of being unable to work.

The injured employee must request the leave per company leave policy.

If the insurance carrier is obligated to reimburse for the first

days of disability (if certain circumstances provide for

reimbursement), the reimbursement will be paid directly to the

company and the amount of reimbursement will be used to replace the

leave used for the job injury. Since workers compensation only pays

two-thirds of the employee wages, the amount of leave replaced will

be approximately two-thirds of the leave used (during the first seven

days of disability). If the injured employee has no paid leave

available, the company is not obligated to advance any benefits

to the injured employee.

9. Any insurance coverages or other special deductions (other than standard

deductions) deducted from the injured employees paycheck, will be the

responsibility of the injured employee while that employee is receiving

lost time benefits from the workers' compensation insurance carrier.

10. It is important that all employees understand that the workers'

compensation insurance carrier and not your company has control of the claim and benefits once the claim is filed for a job injury.

NOTE: The policy example is a start; you must check your state rules regarding what you can or cannot require your employees to do.

PREMIUM HELP FOR BUSINESSES:

In order to make sure the workers' compensation premium does not place an undue hardship on the budget of business, certain steps can be taken once the business understands the basics of the premium calculation.

Workers' compensation premiums are calculated based on the risk and payroll of a job category or group. For purposes of premium calculation, all employees of the same risk or job classifications are lumped together and the total payroll for those employees is determined.

The payroll for the group is then multiplied times the rate (determined by accidents for similar groups in your area or state, and associated costs). The result is a basic premium sometimes called the "manual premium" since the rates and calculations come from the "regulation manual". The same procedure is done for all groups or job classifications in a business until all payroll is accounted for within a group or classification. The premiums are added together for all groups to obtain a total "manual premium" for the business for a particular premium year.

If the business is large enough to qualify for an experience rating, the experience modifier is calculated and is then multiplied times the manual premium. If the experience modifier is below 1.00, the premium is discounted by the percentage (example, an experience modifier of .80 would result in a 20% discount from the manual premium). If the experience modifier is above 1.00, the manual premium is increased by the percentage (example, an experience modifier of 1.20 would result in a penalty of 20% of the manual premium). 1.00 is average for an experience modifier, below 1.00 is good, above 1.00 is not good.

The modified premium (including the ARAP for assigned risk businesses) is the premium a business is required to pay.

One major problem is that the insurance carrier must estimate the premium a year in advance based on several factors which are not known at the time of the premium estimate. The advance estimate is the reason Insurance Carriers sometimes ask for additional

premium on a past year the following year. The unknown

factors include:

1. Actual approved rates for the estimated premium year (the rates

may change higher or lower after the premium estimates are sent).

2. The experience modifier may change (actual total losses are not

available for the premium year that is being estimated).

3. The expected loss rates used in the estimated experience

modifier calculation may change in the middle of the premium period.

4. Payroll may change for the business. The addition of employees

or a reduction in payroll WILL affect the premium estimate since

the payroll amount used for the estimate is no longer valid.

5. Amounts paid on claims used in the experience modifier

calculation may change dramatically which causes the experience

modifier to increase or decrease drastically since it is based

on claims losses and amounts paid on claims (example, a simple claim may "go bad" resulting in a large claim loss. Since the insurance carrier could not foresee that event, the "reserve" or estimated loss amount for that claim must be increased which will affect the experience modifier and therefore the premium.

As you can see, the estimated premiums sent to businesses at the beginning of the policy period can be inaccurate. It is for this reason that the insurance carrier "audits" businesses. The main purpose of the audit is to make sure the premium amount estimated for the year being audited was in fact accurate. During the premium audit, ACTUAL rates, payroll, and a final calculated experience modifier are used for an accurate premium estimate. Once the audit is done, the premium for the audited year is generally final.

The "audited premium" will result in the business paying more money to the insurance carrier for the premium year (debit) or a refund to the business for the amount overcharged by the carrier (credit). It is the large debit which hurts the business since the amounts can cause a great hardship, but like taxes, the amount must be paid in general when due.

There are several actions a business can take to help minimize any large fluctuations in the premium and the resulting affect on the budget of the business:

1. It is a good idea to include an additional amount in the budget for the workers' compensation premium. 10% additional is a minimum with a higher figure needed if there has been a severe accident or large increases in payroll or risky jobs at the business. If the business can afford it, budgeting for 20% additional to the estimated premium for a given year is not a bad idea. If not needed, the result is additional funds for the business after the premium audit.

2. Make sure payroll records are absolutely accurate and do not understate or overstate payroll. The carrier will check the payroll to verify amounts and will check those against federal payroll reporting.

3. Workers should be classified in the least risky job category they can be logically placed in. This must be discussed with

the carrier, but the carrier does at times make mistakes and

place workers in a higher risk category by mistake which

increases the premium. Time taken here to explain the job

descriptions with the auditor from the carrier can pay off

if you suspect the worker(s) is wrongly classified.

4. Keep accurate overtime and payroll records, by employee.

Send the payroll listing to the carrier when requested

and include overtime payroll BY EACH EMPLOYEE.

5. If you have a strong safety program, or something has

changed in the business which will result in fewer accidents

or risk, NOTIFY THE CARRIER for a possible change in the

premium estimate or other positive actions by the carrier.

6. When an audited premium is received by a business, someone

with skills should check the audit for accuracy and discuss

the audit with a carrier representative.

7. If your business is in the assigned risk pool, shop around.

there is a remote possibility the business could be accepted in the voluntary market (lower premiums). If a particular agent or company cannot provide a source of voluntary coverage, check with another agent or an association for group rates.

8. Spend the necessary funds to start and maintain a good accident reduction program. Hire an outside consultant if needed. Money spent here pays dividends.

9. Ask your insurance carrier if you can make installment payments on the premium (quarterly as an example). This will allow the funds to collect interest before they are used to pay for the premium.

10. Always cooperate with the carrier requests, loss prevention representatives, auditors, claims representatives, and others from the insurance carrier. It is not a good idea to "get into a fight" with those representatives. The loss prevention people are there to help you reduce your accidents (and premiums!). Making the auditors angry could result in workers being classified in a higher category, if there are several acceptable categories. Claims representatives set the reserves on your claims. Reserves

affect the experience modifier and therefore the premium. You should

help the claims representative close any claims for your workers

as soon as possible. If you are abusive to the claims representative

the odds of your claims being handled as a priority are slim to none.

Work with the insurance representatives, not against them.

11. If your business plans to increase staff, pay, or benefits (leave

time, autos, etc.) make sure you budget for the associated increases

in the workers' compensation premium. Some businesses do not take

the premium increases into account and end up paying the price by

having to use other funds to pay the audited premium increase.

12. If your business has an increase in the number of accidents,

the severity of accidents, or a claim looks like it will end

up costing a large amount of money, plan to see an increase in

your premium in the next year(s) and budget accordingly. Keep

track of your claims and look for trends. There is no excuse

to be caught off-guard with respect to increased experience

modifiers and premiums due to accidents.

13. Always remember, the insurance carrier would rather not

increase the premium since it means the carrier is having

to pay more for claims losses or is assuming more risk. It

is for that reason that "jumping" from carrier to carrier is

not a good idea in the long run and will most likely hurt

the ability of a business to obtain the best coverage at the

best price. Insurance carriers do not like "jumpers".

BE AWARE OF THIS BEFORE BARGAIN SHOPPING EACH YEAR.

14.No matter how cheap the premium estimate is, you may be

"hit" with a large audited premium (low-balling to obtain

coverage). It is also important to note that a lack of proper

services by the insurance carrier can result in a higher

premium in the long run. A carrier who does not properly

handle any claims a business may have will do a large amount

of damage to the premium costs for the business since the

experience modifier is based also on amounts paid. The

experience modifier is "attached" to the business and goes

to each carrier the business selects. A lack of loss prevention

services are no bargain even if the premium is cheaper. Use

common sense and remember the saying "pay me now or pay

me later" or "you get what you pay for".

One of the most important parts of the workers' compensation premium is the experience rating factor. The experience rating is basically a way for the insurance carrier to "reward" businesses with low losses (claims) and to "punish" businesses with high losses (claims). The experience rating factor also allows the insurance carrier to cover unexpected losses by increasing the premium AFTER the losses have occurred. The whole process can be thought of as similar to automobile rating. If a driver has an accident or two, the premium increases. If a driver has no accidents, the premium does not really increase and the safe driver may get a dividend or discount. The same process holds true for workers' compensation coverage.

While the rate charged for each job category is a major factor in the premium amount, the experience modifier is the real culprit when it comes to those "unexpected" and large premium increases from one year to the next. To fully understand the process, would take a scientist or actuary.

The process can be explained in overly simple, but understandable terms using examples based on actual regulations in some areas of the country.

EXPERIENCE RATING PROCESS:

1. Payroll and expected losses

A. In addition to using payroll for the basic premium, it is also used
for the experience rating process. For each job description
(such as "Heavy Equipment Operator") there is an expected amount of
losses based on all employees in a state with that job description.
From loss statistics, a rate or percentage of payroll figure is
calculated which says in effect " If you have someone working this job,
expect to have X% of payroll in claims payments". The insurance carrier
multiplies each job description (or group of similar jobs) payroll times
the expected loss rate and comes up with a total amount of expected
claim losses for that particular group of employees based on total payroll.
The same procedure is carried out for all groups of employees until
every employee is used in the expected claim loss calculation.

The result is the total expected claims losses for a company.

Remember, the loss figures come from the combined losses of all of the businesses with the similar jobs in the rating area (geographic such as state).

EXAMPLE:

EXPECTED LOSS RATE X PAYROLL = EXPECTED LOSS

2. Allowance for huge accidents.

A. It would not be fair to "hit" the premium of a company which suffered a large unexpected loss, such as a fatal injury or other tragic event resulting in a severe and expensive claim. It is recognized that some large accidents may happen to the best companies. Since most companies would not be able to absorb a huge premium increase from a tragic event, one total amount of losses used in the experience rating (called ACTUAL PRIMARY LOSSES) process is capped at a certain amount per claim. In other words a claim may cost $ 250,000 but the amount used in the actual primary loss calculation process may be limited to a maximum. There is a formula for this and the actual amount "charged" for losses may vary based on current

116

rating rules.

THE IMPORTANCE OF THE ACTUAL PRIMARY LOSS VALUE IS AS
FOLLOWS:

The primary loss amounts are more indicative of frequency of accidents.
It is far more harmful to the experience modifier for a business to
have a large number of small accidents, than a single injury with
large losses. It should be pointed out that the larger a company is,
the more effect "large" accidents have on the experience modifier.

It is for this reason that a company should reduce or eliminate
the large number of accidents, even if they are minor. The potential
large accident should be prevented if possible, but companies should
do everything (especially small companies) they can to reduce the
frequency of worker accidents and injuries.

The reason a large number of small accidents is so important, is
that to the insurance carrier every open claim of any size has the
potential to turn into a "bad" or high loss claim. A large number
of small accidents also indicates a lack of company control over

safety and potential injuries. A large number of accidents during

a given period of time is like a "red flag" and indicates

a DANGEROUS work environment that is out of control!

EXAMPLE: ACTUAL PRIMARY LOSS FUNCTION OF EXPERIENCE

MODIFIER

PRIMARY LOSS AMOUNT MAXIMUM PER CLAIM = $10,000

LOSS ON A PARTICULAR CLAIM IS $100,000

PRIMARY LOSS USED IN EXPERIENCE CALCULATION MAY BE

LIMITED TO $10,000 FOR THAT PARTICULAR CLAIM (CHECK YOUR

STATE RATING RULES).

B. Losses up to $ 2,000 for example, are charged at the actual amount

and the formula is not used. To put it simple, a single large accident

is reduced for primary losses according to the rules.

Small accidents up to $ 2,000 in losses are included at the loss

value without any changes or reductions of full value.

EXAMPLE:

ACTUAL LOSS AMOUNT ON A CLAIM = $1,500

AMOUNT USED IN EXPERIENCE CALCULATION = $ 1,500

3. Importance of ACTUAL INCURRED LOSSES:

It would not be statistically valid to only use frequency as a

measure of the risk of a business. The other loss figure used

in the experience modifier calculation is the ACTUAL INCURRED

LOSS figure. This figure represents the estimated TOTAL cost

for a claim to conclusion. While only a small amount may be

PAID at the time of the calculation, the estimated value is

used for the experience modifier calculation.

EXAMPLE:

AMOUNT ACTUALLY PAID ON CLAIM AS OF CALCULATION $ 4,000

RESERVED AMOUNT (expected total cost of claim) $ 100,000

AMOUNT USED FOR ACTUAL INCURRED LOSS $ 100,000

This reserve process does confuse many people. The amount paid on a claim is NOT the same as the reserve or ultimate loss value of the claim. The reserved amount is the amount the carrier expects to pay by the time the claim is concluded and closed. Actually the amount paid as of any date is of little value unless the claim is closed. The more important amount is what is EXPECTED to be paid (insurance carriers must budget for all claims payments to remain solvent). If the claim is closed during the rating period for the experience modifier (example 3 years) and the claim costs less, the reserve amount is reduced to the actual loss and this would reduce your experience modifier and premium.

IMPORTANT NOTE:

NOTE: As stated above, the formula takes into account the size of a business and in some instances, the large single claim loss may have little or NO EFFECT on the experience modifier of a small business. Remember, a business who has a large number of claims of any size is less attractive to Insurance Carriers than a business that has a single large accident!

4. How it all works together to increase or decrease the premium:

To put it as simple as possible, the calculations are all done and an expected loss amount is calculated for each company (the experience rating process rates each company individually) for a particular premium period. If the company has more claim losses for that year than expected (based on the calculations) the experience modifier increases. If the company has less claim losses than expected (based on the calculations) the experience modifier decreases. The whole thing can be thought of as a type of budget process. Each company with an experience rating is "budgeted" a certain amount of losses by the insurance carrier based on statistics. If the company exceeds the "budget" the premium is increased (just as if you exceeded your budget in the business and had to borrow more money to pay the difference). If the company uses less than the "budget" of losses, the premium is decreased (like having a great year in your business and paying off a loan resulting in less business costs).

EXAMPLE: EXPECTED LOSSES (EXPECTED AND PRIMARY)

ACTUAL LOSSES   (INCURRED AND PRIMARY)

ACTUAL LOSSES/EXPECTED LOSSES = EXPERIENCE MODIFIER

COMPANY A:

EXPECTED LOSSES = 50,000

ACTUAL LOSSES   = 50,000

50,000/50,000 = 1.00 EXPERIENCE MODIFIER = 1.00 *

COMPANY B:

EXPECTED LOSSES = 50,000

ACTUAL LOSSES   = 90,000

90,000/50,000 = 1.80 EXPERIENCE MODIFIER = 1.80 *

COMPANY C:

EXPECTED LOSSES = 50,000

ACTUAL LOSSES =   40,000

40,000/50,000 = .80   EXPERIENCE MODIFIER = .80 *

* The formula is extremely complicated and has many

adjustments and balances. This example is overly

simple but does make the point rather clear.

IMPORTANT:

There is one thing all businesses of which businesses should be aware.

Every claim affects the experience rating process for THREE (3)

years (in most areas but this may vary in your area depending on

rating rules).

The three year time period means businesses with low losses will reap the

benefits for years to come, but businesses with high claims losses will pay the

price for years to come. This is a main reason it is so hard to reduce a premium once a high experience rating is attached to a business. IT TAKES YEARS, even after a good safety program is started. The good news is that the premium increase for a "bad" year in claims, is spread over a longer time period so the business does not have to pay the increased premium all in one year. On the other hand, if a business has a great year with no claims losses, losses in the next two years would be somewhat helped (with respect to a premium increase) and the effect of the losses would be "watered down" by the great year.

ASSIGNED RISK VERSES VOLUNTARY COVERAGE: ARAP

While the calculation method may vary for the assigned risk verses the voluntary market, and the losses allowed may differ in the two types of coverage, the principle is basically the same. Companies who have higher than expected claims will pay a penalty and companies with lower than expected claims will be rewarded with a type of discount. With the assigned risk adjustment program (ARAP), businesses in the assigned risk pool with larger than expected losses are also charged an additional penalty for having higher than expected claims losses even in the assigned risk pool! The ARAP penalty is added to the experience modifier adjustment. When you add the higher rates in the assigned risk pool, the claims experience modifier, and the ARAP penalty, assigned risk premiums can really get expensive compared to the voluntary market. Being in the assigned risk pool is expensive!

SOME WAYS TO REDUCE THE WORKERS' COMPENSATION PREMIUM:

1. Make sure the insurance carrier has your employees classified properly and is not charging you for a higher risk employee. Premium audits should show the employee classification information and you have the right to ask for the classification and premium cost for each class of worker or each worker individually.

2. Keep accurate overtime records and list the overtime separately in the payroll listing you send to the insurance carrier. List each employee's overtime separately. In most cases you will pay more premium if the overtime is simply listed in with the total payroll figures and not broken down by employee.

3. Start a strong safety program and make a commitment to continue the program. Notify your insurance carrier that you have a strong safety program and ask for a discount.

4. Select a designated physician for treatment of injured employees (try to negotiate a fixed price per employee treated as an initial

visit. Some physicians will do this.) Note : some states may not allow the employer to choose the physician, most do.

5. If you have an open claim, keep track of the claim and do everything you can to assist the carrier with closing the claim. Follow up with the physicians and the injured employee to see how things are going. Offer light duty work when the physician approves light duty. Stay in contact with the adjuster handling your employee's claim and let the Adjusters know you are watching the way the claim is being handled. IT IS YOUR MONEY TOO!

6. Don't "punish" workers who are injured on the job. In the long run, such actions have proven to cost more not less! Try to show the injured worker you care and do everything you can to help the worker. MOST injured workers who go to an attorney do so because they feel the company did not care enough about them after they were injured on the job, NOT BECAUSE THEY THINK THEY CAN GET MORE MONEY.

7. Learn the laws of your state and obey them. Fines assessed to businesses on workers' compensation matters can be very expensive and NOT covered by insurance.

8. Try to do everything you can to make sure any claim goes smooth and without unnecessary delays. Handled properly by the employer and Carrier, a claim can be closed quickly and with less cost or increase in premium due the experience modifier calculation.

9. Review the audit sent to you by the insurance carrier. Even though the audit forms look complicated; they can be understood and reviewed for mistakes. Everyone makes mistakes now and then. If you discover an error it can save you on your premium costs for Workers' Compensation coverage.

10. If you have had bad claims losses, and you have taken action to permanently correct the problem (such as a good safety program) let your agent or insurance carrier know as it could result in a lower premium next time you are up for renewal (or may be the difference in being placed in the more expensive assigned risk pool or not).

11. Keep detailed records of any pre-existing medical problems which you are aware of when hiring an employee, or after the employee is employed by you. Some states have a fund that helps reimburse the carrier for payments made on a person with a pre-existing medical problem which

made the injury worse. Any reduction in the amount paid on one of your claims will affect your premium costs. Be careful not to violate ADA rules regarding discrimination against people with health conditions.

12. You may wish to request a copy of all bills related to a claims of your injured employees. Check the bills for accuracy and notify the carrier if you find an error or overcharge. FOLLOW UP TO MAKE SURE THE OVER CHARGES WERE CORRECTED as the amount paid on claims affects your premium.

13. Treat your workers' compensation premium just as you would any other bill sent to you. You do not have to simply pay the insurance premium bill and forget about it. Workers' compensation premiums can be reduced by many ways if you know how. Remember, workers' compensation coverage may be required, but you still have some rights with regard to what you can do. If needed, call in an experienced consultant to assist you with ways to reduce your Workers' Compensation premium cost.

14. Workers' compensation costs can be reduced if any company makes the

effort and is willing to spend the time. Money spent in the area of reducing Workers' Compensation premiums and work related injuries usually pays back in large multiples of what was spent.

INJURY REDUCTION

The key to reducing injuries is of course to reduce accidents

and the things that cause the accidents. It is not as hard

as it might seem to reduce accidents.

Accident reduction suggestions:

1. Properly train all employees in the use of safety equipment.

2. Enforce safety rules and regulations.

3. Provide proper safety equipment and enforce their proper use.

4. Do not allow removal of any safety devices from or modifications of company

equipment.

5. Set up a safety program with proper compliance monitoring.

6. Keep the work place free of possible hazards and have regular internal

inspections.

7. Train employees to report or remove any possible safety hazard IMMEDIATELY.

8. Obtain information from regulatory authorities on safety requirements for the business.

9. Ask for a safety survey from your workers' compensation carrier.

10. Set up a formal safety policy for employees and enforce the policy.

11. Make sure all management is committed to safety and supports safety policy; it must begin at the top to be effective.

12. Train employees in first aid procedures.

13. It something appears too risky, don't allow it under any circumstances.

14. Discipline the supervisor as well as the worker for failure to follow proper safety procedures.

15.Never punish a worker who points out safety problems.

16.Nothing is too small to deal with, some of the worst accidents happen from small safety problems.

17.Budget funds for safety devices and programs, they are important to the business.

18.Join safety groups or associations for expert help.

19.Subscribe to trade publications that include safety tips for your type of business.

20.Seek outside consulting help if you are not sure.

21.Remember, managers have gone to jail for extreme violations of OSHA rules and negligence.

22.Make sure all safety rules and requirements are complied with for your local area in addition to other rules (codes etc.).

23.If funds are available, hire a part or full time safety expert for your business.

24.Do not permit "horseplay" in the workplace.

25.A regular internal inspection of all equipment is a must.

26.BE SAFE, IT IS LIKE MONEY IN THE BANK.

The following forms are examples of useful forms to help reduce Accidents and reduce your premium through experience modifier reduction.

Since laws are different in all states (Workers' Compensation is State Law not Federal Law) check with your regulatory agency to make sure use of these forms or any part of them is not a violation of the rules of your state. Before you use these forms you should also check with your Workers' Compensation insurance carrier for suggestions they may offer you.

Be careful with the information you collect on employee injuries or accidents so as not to violate their privacy rights.

The forms are © Mark Kirby however as the owner of this book you are granted rights to remove the pages from the book, copy them, and use them in your business. Please do not give blank copies of the forms to other companies to use or let them copy the forms as that is a violation of the copyright.

SUPERVISOR JOB INJURY AND SAFETY

REPORT FOR INTERNAL USE

COMPANY NAME_____

NAME OF SUPERVISOR_____

 EMPLOYEE INJURED ON DATE_____ TIME_____

ON WORK PREMISES? YES___ NO___

IF NOT ON PREMISES:

LOCATION_____

_____

NAME OF INJURED

EMPLOYEE(S)_____

_____

JOB POSITION(S) OF

INJURED_____

_____

_____

WHAT WAS EMPLOYEE DOING WHEN ACCIDENT

HAPPENED_____

_____

_____

_____

_____

NAMES OF

WITNESSES_____

_____

_____

WAS EMPLOYEE PERFORMING THEIR USUAL DUTIES WHEN INJURED?

YES___ NO___ IF NOT WHAT WERE THEY DOING_____

_____

WAS ANYTHING UNUSUAL NOTICED BY ANYONE BEFORE OR AFTER

THE ACCIDENT?

_____

_____

_____

WHEN DID THE EMPLOYER FIRST KNOW ABOUT THE ACCIDENT

DATE_____ TIME_____

HOW DID SUPERVISOR FIND OUT ABOUT THE ACCIDENT?

_____

_____

_____

_____

_____

_____

WHEN DID INJURED EMPLOYEE NOTIFY YOU?

DATE_____ TIME_____

HOW DID THE INJURED EMPLOYEE NOTIFY YOU?

_____

_____

_____

NOTE ANY IMPORTANT FACTS OR DETAIL HERE:

_____

_____

_____

_____

_____

WHAT SINGLE THING MOST LIKEY CAUSED THE ACCIDENT?

_____

_____

_____

_____

DID INJURY REQUIRE (CHECK ALL THAT APPLY):

FIRST AID___ DOCTOR TREATMENT___ HOSPITAL___

TRANSPORT BY ABULANCE ___

WILL TIME OFF FROM WORK BE REQUIRED

NO___ YES___ AMOUNT____(DAYS)

IF OFF FROM WORK, EMPLOYEE IS EXPECTED TO RETURN ON

DATE_____

WAS THE CAUSE OF ACCIDENT CORRECTED ___YES ___NO. IF YES,

DATE_____

IF THE ACCIDENT CAUSE WAS NOT CORRECTED, WHY?

_____

_____

HOW LONG HAD INJURED EMPLOYEE BEEN WORKING FOR COMPANY

WHEN INJURED?

_____YEARS _____ MONTHS _____DAYS.

PART TIME____ FULL TIME____

IS THIS THE FIRST ACCIDENT REPORTED BY EMPLOYEE? ____YES

____NO

LIST ANY OTHER ACCIDENT DATES AND TYPES FOR THIS EMPLOYEE IF

APPLICABLE :

_____

_____

_____

_____

SIGNED (SUPERVISOR)_____ DATE_____

JOB INJURY TRACKING FORM FOR INTERNAL USE

COMPANY NAME_____

EMPLOYEE NAME_____

EMPLOYEE SSN_____

DATE OF INJURY_____TIME_____DAY_____

WITNESS

NAMES_____

_____

_____

NAME OF INSURANCE CARRIER:

_____PHONE_____

CARRIER NOTIFIED_____(DATE)

_____

INJURY REPORT SENT ON_____(DATE)

CARRIER CLAIM ADJUSTOR'S NAME_____

DIRECT PHONE_____

NOTICE OF CLAIM

ACCEPTANCE_____ DENIAL_____

RECEIVED ON DATE_____

IF DENIED:

REASON_____

_____

_____

_____

CLAIMANT ATTORNEY NAME_____

PHONE_____

CARRIER/DEFENSE ATTORNEY NAME_____

PHONE_____

YOUR COMPANY ATTORNEY

NAME_____PHONE_____

HEARING SCHEDULED _____YES _____NO

DATE_____ TIME_____

HEARING LOCATION

_____

_____

_____

_____

INFORMATION REQUESTED BY DEFENSE ATTORNEY

(The attorney representing YOU or your carrier)

_____

_____SENT ON (DATE)_____

AND_____AND_____AND_____.

EMPLOYEE BEING TREATED BY

DR._____

PHONE NUMBER _____

LOST TIME ____YES ____NO

EXCUSE FROM DR._____FOR____DAYS

DATE EMPLOYEE TO RETURN TO WORK_____ ON EXCUSE

DATED_____

EMPLOYEE RETURNED TO WORK ____PARTIAL ____ FULL DUTIES ON

(DATE) _____

CARRIER NOTIFIED (DATE)_____ THAT EMPLOYEE RETURNED

TO WORK (DATE) _____

(CARRIER SHOULD BE NOTIFIED 2 WEEKS IN ADVANCE OF RETURN TO WORK TO AVOID OVERPAYMENT OF COMPENSATION)

SIGNED_____

DATE_____

     COMPANY OFFICIAL

COMPLETE THIS FORM IN FULL AND RETAIN FOR YOUR RECORDS

SAFETY AND ACCIDENT PREVENTION FORM

COMPANY NAME_____

THIS FORM MUST BE COMPLETED BY THE INJURED EMPLOYEE <u>AND</u>

THE   SUPERVISOR ONCE AN ACCIDENT OR INJURY IS REPORTED. THE

EMPLOYEE   COMPLETES THE FIRST PART, THE SUPERVISOR

COMPLETES SECOND PART.

EMPLOYEE PART ONE

MY JOB ACCIDENT ON _____(DATE) WAS CAUSED MOSTLY BY:

_____

_____

_____

_____

_____

TO PREVENT A SIMILAR ACCIDENT THE COMPANY NEEDS TO:

_____

_____

_____

_____

THE CAUSE OF THE ACCIDENT WAS REPORTED

TO_____AND I FOLLOWED UP

ON_____(DATE) TO MAKE SURE THE PROBLEM WAS CORRECTED,

AND IT WAS___ WAS NOT___ CORRECTED. IF NOT WHY?

_____

_____

_____

_____ DATE_____

    EMPLOYEE

SAFETY AND ACCIDENT PREVENTION FORM

SUPERVISOR **PART TWO**

COMPANY NAME_____

THIS FORM MUST BE COMPLETED BY THE INJURED EMPLOYEE <u>AND</u>

THE SUPERVISOR ONCE AN ACCIDENT OR INJURY IS REPORTED. THE

EMPLOYEE COMPLETES THE FIRST PART, THE SUPERVISOR

COMPLETES SECOND PART.

THE SAFETY PROBLEM RELATED TO THE ACCIDENT ON

DATE_____

 WAS REPORTED TO ME ON

DATE_____BY_____

THE FOLLOWING ACTION(S) WERE TAKEN TO PREVENT ANOTHER

ACCIDENT_____

_____

_____

_____

EMPLOYEE INPUT IN TO PREVENTING FUTURE ACCIDENTS

_____

_____

_____

SIGNED SUPERVISOR_____

DATE_____

(OR SAFETY DIRECTOR)

THE SAFETY COMMITTEE HAS BEEN NOTIFIED   DATE_____

SAFETY COMMITTEE REVIEWED PROBLEM ON   DATE_____

SAFETY COMMITTEE ENACTED SOLUTION ON   DATE_____

TERMS AND MEANINGS:

APPEAL: requesting another decision on the claim.

CARRIER: a company who must pay for job injuries, insurance
Company that is paid a premium and "carries" the risk.

CLAIM: asking for benefits due to an accident.

COMMISSIONER: a type of non-court judge for workers' compensation matters.

DISABILITY: a damaged part of the body that will never
heal to 100% of what it was before the injury.

DOCKET: a number given to appeals and court cases to keep track
of them

EMERGENCY: an accident that requires immediate hospital
treatment.

FILING A CLAIM: asking for benefits to be paid relating to an accident.

FEES: costs paid to an attorney for work done.

FRAUD: misleading people to get money you are not entitled to.

LOST WAGES: not getting paid because you are unable to work due
to an accident.

REPORTING AN ACCIDENT: The process of an injured employee telling the
employer
they have been injured on the job.

SELF INSURANCE: where a business covers itself for claim
losses (no carrier) but may include some type of excess loss coverage from an
insurance carrier for large claims or losses.

STATE FUND: a semi-state agency that is a carrier for
Workers' Compensation.

ABOUT THE AUTHOR:

Mark Kirby is a recognized Workers' Compensation expert with almost thirty years experience in the field of Workers' Compensation including;

- Investigations

- Management

- Actuarial and Premium calculation

- Computer program automation of premium calculation and the claims handling and reserving process.

Mr. Kirby has also been published in an international insurance publication and has given many lectures on Worker's Compensation. Businesses and agencies both have credited Mr. Kirby with saving their business due to Workers' Compensation issues or greatly reducing their Workers' Compensation premium costs.

Mr. Kirby was also greatly instrumental in rescuing an insolvent Insurance Carrier and changing the 30 million dollar shortfall in the claims fund to a surplus.

Always remember, your employees are your most valuable company assets and when they are injured you should treat them as you would treat your own family members. Show you care about your employees and it will pay benefits for your company.